War Zone

poems by

Michael Miller

Finishing Line Press
Georgetown, Kentucky

War Zone

Copyright © 2025 by Michael Miller
ISBN 979-8-89990-106-5 First Edition
All rights reserved under International and Pan-American Copyright Conventions. No part of this book may be reproduced in any manner whatsoever without written permission from the publisher, except in the case of brief quotations embodied in critical articles and reviews.

Publisher: Leah Huete de Maines
Editor: Christen Kincaid
Author Photo: Mary Miller
Cover Design: Elizabeth Maines McCleavy

Order online: www.finishinglinepress.com
also available on amazon.com

> Author inquiries and mail orders:
> Finishing Line Press
> PO Box 1626
> Georgetown, Kentucky 40324
> USA

Contents

I

Scarred 1
What He Trained For 2
Uprisings of Memory 3
Ticking 4
Woodpecker 5
Walking Point 6
The Angry Lieutenant 7
The Leeches 8
The Machine-Gun 9
Grunt 10
Shrapnel 11
The Duffel Bag 12
Platoon Leader 13
Alone 14

II

The Corpsman 19

III

A View From The Infantry 39
The Sergeant 40
The Youngest Private 41
On The Chopper 42
Patrol 43

The Left Trail	44
You Never Hear…	45
The Stray Bullet	46
Ten Days And A Wake-up	47
Bad Memories	48
The Beard	49
The Face In The Mirror	50
Brothers	51
Three Bullets	52
Turning Away	53
Encounter	54
In The Veteran's Home	55

*For those who served in Vietnam,
the living and the dead.*

I

SCARRED

With the tenderness of
His scarred right hand,
The hand he rarely
Offered to anyone,
He stroked the white head
Of his neighbor's goat
As he looked into its eyes.
This was the communion
That nothing at the VA
Could provide, this was
The peace healing his wounds,
The other side of war
He had finally found.

WHAT HE TRAINED FOR

Boredom brought
The next mission closer,
The long awaited
Adrenalin rush in combat,
The firepower exchanged
In the bush or the hills
Where he would live or die
With medals of blood.
This is what he trained for
At Parris Island,
A young Marine with innocence
To be given, to be lost.

UPRISINGS OF MEMORY

We needed a replacement for God,
God had allowed Reardon
To be tied to a stake
And castrated.

Decades have passed;
Vietnam remains vivid
In uprisings of memory:
Burnett stepping on a landmine,
Riggins and McAlpine
Cut down in a crossfire,
The recklessness of lieutenants,
The mistakes of generals.

Why not be done with
His incriminating ghosts,
His morbid wait for death?
Would he feel release
Gripping his straight razor,
Cutting railroad tracks
Across his wrists?

Bound to the knowledge of blood
He is not ready to die.
He will continue
To honor his men
In thoughts, in deed;
His annual visit
To that long black wall,
His fingers moving
Quietly across the names
In the stone.

TICKING

A gray-haired man
With scars and tattoos
Wakes from the loud ticking
Of a bomb under his bed,
Feels the desolation
Of being alone
In a war zone of the night.
Sitting up quickly,
Peering through the dark,
Listening with fear
Driving his alertness,
All he hears is silence,
Imagines body parts
Scattered in the room.
Enough, he thinks,
And realizes again
A woman must rescue him,
His disguised need
For love now revealed.
Help me, he thinks,
Extending his hand.

WOODPECKER

Sergeant Hodges was the first
To call him Woodpecker.
He tapped on wood
Before every mission,
Tapped on the nearest tree,
A sharpshooter who wanted
That extra bit of luck.

He returned to West Virginia
With the Bronze Star
And without a scratch.
Tapping remained
A part of his life.
Nobody in the coal mine
Called him Woodpecker
When he tapped on a beam.

Since turning eighty
He taps the table louder
When his wife mentions cancer.
Because he wants them
To live to ninety
He taps nine times
Every morning, hoping to see
Nine birds at sunrise.

WALKING POINT

The cigarette smoke
Clinging to his clothes
Is always with him
Like the memory of trip wires,
Of bodies exploding,
Of ambushes in the jungle
Where spiders
As large as his hand
Crawled from the rocks.
He had nowhere to hide,
A young Marine walking point
On a patrol he feared
Would be his last.
Vietnam has never ended:
The stutter of rifle fire
Reverberates in his dreams,
A crow calling reminds him
Of the cry, "Corpsman, corpsman!"
On his license plate:
<u>Disabled Veteran,</u>
A snake of scar
Curves down his leg,
His four-pronged black cane
A memorial to his comrades.

THE ANGRY LIEUTENANT

First in his class at Annapolis,
His pride stood at attention
When he chose to serve
In the Marine Corps.
Everything changed in Vietnam:
The dysfunctional
Chain of command,
The senseless missions,
The obsession with body counts.
Semper fidelis, esprit de corps,
Words that evoked his anger.
Discharged with honor,
Returning to Pennsylvania,
He buried his anger
With seeds in his garden.

THE LEECHES

He peels them off,
The leeches on his left arm.
A VC sniper moves
Through the foliage
Seeking the right place
For the perfect shot,
A bullet tearing
Through the photograph
Of his wife and daughter
In the pocket over his heart.
All this he imagines,
His death the clinging leech
He will burn off,
Lighting a cigarette,
Determined to return home.

THE MACHINE-GUN

When the firefight ended
He never thought about
The VC he had killed,
His machine-gun
A continuous spit of bullets,
His pumped-up eighteen years
Gradually slowing down.
All he wanted to do
Was clean and kiss
His machine-gun.

GRUNT

Navigating the jagged edges
Of combat, he felt
The short-timer's pride
Of being called grunt,
His modesty in check
Because of the up close
Dying he had seen.
Carelessness had no place
In a firefight,
Fear brought out
His drive to survive.

SHRAPNEL

Lying still as pain shuffles
Through his legs
The decades rush backwards
Until he is in the field hospital
With shrapnel in both legs.
The Marine beside him
Is talking to his mother
Who isn't there,
Telling her his wound is minor
And he will soon be home,
Never mentioning the bandage
Wrapped around his head,
Covering his eyes.
The past, the present—
He never knew
If the Marine was blind.
In his top dresser drawer
He keeps the five pieces
Of shrapnel removed from his legs.
He never questions why
He keeps them with his socks
Where he can see them every day.

THE DUFFEL BAG

In his duffel bag
He stuffed his life,
The letters from his wife,
His daughter's crayon drawings,
The books he wanted to read,
A corpsman finished
With his training
Ready for Vietnam.
Now his duffel bag
Is folded neatly
In the attic under the dust.
The past remains
In the present
Waiting to be remembered.
Every time he washes his hands
He looks for blood,
The men whose lives
He saved, the men
Who died in his arms.

PLATOON LEADER

Readying his platoon for combat
He felt summoned by
The texture of leadership:
Preparation, knowledge, instinct.
He considered his men,
Never lost sight
Of the mission,
Chose the tangles of foliage
Instead of the trail with
Booby traps, land mines.
He wanted to bring his men home:
Some would die, he might die.
Fear was always present,
Fear faced, fear controlled.
Cowardice, unacceptable.

ALONE

An old man alone
Misses the kindness
Of the nurses at the VA,
Calls his comrade in Seattle
To talk about Vietnam.

An old man alone
Regrets the shutting down
Of marriage, his quick temper
Escalating their disagreements,
Her slowness to forgive.

An old man alone
Kisses the photograph of his mother
Who died too soon,
Wears a suit and tie
On his birthday.

An old man alone
Irons the wrinkles out of his uniform
But not the memories of war,
Moves his fingers along the ridge
Of scar across his shoulder.

An old man alone
Never looks at his Purple Heart
In the rectangular box
In his bottom drawer
Beneath the photograph album.

An old man alone
Walks down the road
As rain pocks the dirt,
Looks for a trip wire,
The sniper in the bush.

An old man alone
Feels ashamed to eat
In a restaurant without a friend,
Makes lamb stew
Last for a week.

An old man alone
Sets the table for three,
Lights a candle,
Pours the wine,
Toasts his dead comrades.

An old man alone
Grips the table and shouts,
"I did not want this!"
Reaches for his glass,
Knocks it over and sees blood.

An old man alone
Remembers his once powerful body
That has surrendered to old age,
Imagines death writing his name
In the book of bones.

An old man alone
Leans back in his recliner,
Takes three deep breaths,
Feels his left hand forgive his right,
The hand that had to kill.

An old man alone
Extended his tattooed arms
And said, "Please don't leave,"
As the iron in his spirit vanished—
His wife went out the door.

An old man alone
Going to bed
Combs his white hair—
He would like to die dreaming,
His wife beside him.

II

THE CORPSMAN

I

He tended the shrapnel wound
With all the care
He had acquired,
Working quickly through
The artillery attack,
Determined to save the Marine
After so many deaths
In a war beyond anything
He had imagined—
This was reality,
Stark, indifferent,
Writing its name
In his future.

II

Stop the bleeding,
Plug the holes,
Treat for shock,
The trinity he lived by
For his year in Vietnam,
A Navy corpsman
With the Marines.

III

Incoming mortars
Whistled their preludes
To dismemberment or death.
Now when he hears
A cardinal's call
It carries him back
To the mortars
Before they exploded.

IV

When he rakes the leaves
He thinks of the unread books
Stacked beside his chair.
Raked leaves, books to be read,
Both are part of his life
As autumn yellows toward bareness
And winter will offer
A purity that is not his own.
His innocence was lost in Vietnam.

V

After Vietnam
The years flowed into decades
Taking his wife too soon,
Her memory embedded beside
Those images of Marines
With wounds still calling him
Out of the present
And back to the past.

VI

When he opens the closet
The present becomes the past.
He is the skinny boy
With wide open eyes
In the confessional
Waiting for Father Doyle's
Next question which he
Refuses to answer,
A sinner in his twelfth year
Knowing he can accept
Any punishment without
Saying a word.

VII

Was it Russell Turner
Or Turner Russell?
He cannot remember
The last man's name
He saved in Vietnam.
But his face appears
In his dreams,
His smile containing the fear
As he said, "Save me, Doc."
Working quickly he applied
Pressure to the dressing
And knew he was
Going to save him.

VIII

The accumulating wounds
He treated were transferred
To the hospital of thoughts,
To dreams without conclusions
And letters home
Loaded with lies.

IX

Sometimes he dreamt of napalm,
The gobs sticking to skin,
Burning through fat, muscle, bone.
Men, women, and children
Screamed their way
Into his recurring nightmare.
Waking in a sweat he showered,
Soaping up, letting the cool water
Carry the suds away.

X

His overburdened mind
Creates images of war, of love,
Of the birth of his son,
The death of comrades.
He sees the explosions,
The arterial bleeding
He could not stop.
When his son cut his finger
With his first knife
He cleaned and bandaged it
With the time and gentleness
He never had in combat.

XI

He stopped justifying the war,
Stopped stuffing random death
And death by design
Into the pockets of his soul
That God never emptied.
He was too tired to pray.
He found faith in
The speed of saving a life,
Despair when there was
Nothing more he could do.
But nothing stopped him from
Caring, nothing could harden
His twenty-year-old heart.

XII

He wanted to believe
He was meant to save lives,
Not die young.
He stopped counting on things,
Not even the next cigarette.
In the jungle of doubt
Where the bushes
Held a camouflaged VC
Belief was God
Letting him live to save
A life, giving him
The skill beyond his skills.

XIII

Before his hands
Were used to heal
He loved to draw, to paint:
Crayons, watercolors, oils.
Every Saturday his mother
Drove him to the museum;
He looked carefully
At each painting,
The different faces,
The colors that could
Soothe, disturb.
He never painted
After Vietnam,
He never wore red.

XIV

On a blackboard of the night
Bad memories almost erase good ones.
If only he could halt
A nightmare once it begins,
Open his eyes, close them,
Dream of their son,
His small hands holding their own
As he walked between them
Through a quiet hall
Past the Greek statues in the museum.
What did the Spartans
Say about war,
About gaping abdominal wounds,
Arms ripped off by shrapnel?

XV

Never has he forgotten
The vultures,
A huddle of wings
And bobbing heads picking
At the corpse in the grass,
A memory brought home,
The vultures rising
In his dreams.

XVI

Stacked on a dark shelf
Of memory
The black pages from
A corpsman's calendar of death,
The lives of Marines
He could not save.
Living with death in combat
Kept him on a precipice
That required perfect balance.
Now in the peace
Of his present world
He needs a cane
To keep from falling.

XVII

After the firefight
He treated the wound
And knew it was self-inflicted,
Knew that Milburn had stabbed
His bayonet into his thigh,
Knew he was at a breaking point
And desperate to stay alive,
To avoid another mission.
He saw the fear in Milburn's eyes,
Understood his cowardly act,
Made no accusation.

XVIII

Waking, touching his legs,
His arms, he began to count
The lives he saved,
The lives he lost,
Trying to see
Beyond the wounds,
To focus on the faces,
Some frightened, others
Relieved, each one
A part of himself.

III

A VIEW FROM THE INFANTRY

Each man tried
To step beyond his fear
Before the mission began.
He checked his equipment:
Rifle, ammo, bayonet,
Grenades that seemed
Made for his hand.

A gradual power rose
From within, willing him
To live beyond the shovel
Ready to dig his grave.
We never doubted the power,
He would never know
When it failed.

THE SERGEANT

At dawn he sits at the kitchen table,
Brushing the crumbs away,
Unlocking the vault of his past.
He writes in his forgiving diary,
Releasing the ghosts haunting his dreams,
His men killed in Vietnam.
He is discovering that each word
Leads him to feelings
He had chosen not to confront,
Burying them with his mistakes.

THE YOUNGEST PRIVATE

Innocence marked
His wide-eyed gaze,
His quiet demeanor.
With his Mama's consent
He joined the Marines
At seventeen, the youngest
Private in his platoon.
On patrol in the bush
He dreaded a snake
Gliding toward him,
Dreaded the triangular head,
The deathly grace.
If he died from
A sniper's bullet
He would return to Tennessee
In a Coffin
A snake could never enter.
In his seventh summer
A copperhead bit him,
His ankle swelling
As he ran home,
His Mama there to save him,
His Mama in his thoughts
On patrol.

ON THE CHOPPER

Rotor blades cut through
The heat-stricken air;
The chopper began a slow descent
Onto the field with
Swaying waist-high grass.
First off the chopper
He leapt toward what might be
An ambush with bullets
Stitching across his chest.
Goodbye Vietnam,
Hello body bag
Like a black cocoon.
Goodbye Blue Ridge Mountains,
Mama, Daddy, and Sue Ellen
He wanted to marry.
The chopper rose,
Leaving the squad to fight again.

PATROL

Through the sweating jungle,
Past trees strangled by vines,
They walked silently
Along the narrow trail
With six yards between them,
Alert for the ambush
That never came.
Each step back to base
Brimmed with relief.
He would light up,
Write to his wife,
Hope to see her
As he fell asleep.

THE LEFT TRAIL

Music after midnight
Cannot soothe his soul
When he remembers
Cooper rising up
At Walter Reed to stare at him;
Three surgeries had barely
Changed the map of scars
Across his face.

He was the lieutenant
Who had ordered him
To take the left trail
Where he stepped on a mine.
Decades have not
Changed his guilt,
An accompaniment to the explosion,
A silent one.

YOU NEVER HEAR…

A mild headache, he thought,
Not the one that felt
Like a razor drawn across
His brain that only
A joint could relieve.
They could never get enough
Grass in Vietnam,
Never get stoned enough
To dull the fear
That the next patrol
Would be your last.
Another myth: you never hear
The bullet that kills you.
"I heard it," said Coburn
Bleeding out, his last comrade
To die from a random bullet
That could have been his.

THE STRAY BULLET

In his long night
Of fear, of delusions,
He imagines that if he dies
Suddenly from a stroke
It will be the stray bullet
Meant for him in Vietnam,
Finally come home.

TEN DAYS AND A WAKE-UP

For that year when death
Waited in the bush, the tunnel,
He lived on hope, on prayers,
The letters his wife wrote
Sealed with love he opened carefully.
With ten days and a wake-up
Before his flight home
He felt the bayonet of fear
As his faith grew stronger,
The faith he carried
Closer than his rifle.

BAD MEMORIES

Only the bad memories return:
Full House booby-trapped
And leaving a leg on the trail,
Sideburns pumping bullets
Into a dink dog,
Beanpole holding up
His sliced off hand
And saying, "Look, look."
He never remembers
His wife rushing into his arms
At the Welcome Home Gate,
Pressing her loveliness into him.

THE BEARD

He grew a beard to hide
The scar from shrapnel
On his jaw, a thick beard
As dark as the darkness
The war left in his soul.
He strokes his beard,
Glad that he can
Control its appearance.
The random deaths,
The mistakes, the accidents
Have never left him.

THE FACE IN THE MIRROR

Now, nothing was left to kill except himself.
He had murdered his marriage.
His son's love for him had dissolved.
His friendships of decades were in ruins.

Then, on patrol in the jungle,
He confronted a Cong, fired a burst,
Pumping rounds into the body
As spurts of blood spattered onto his face,
Covered his rifle.

Now, he ate the same breakfast each morning,
Read the same newspaper and took the same walk,
Noticing the squirrel crushed on the road,
The lilies with petals like tongues of gold,
And he hoped something inside him was
Still golden, still waiting to be given
To the right woman if he could find her,
If he could outlast his demons
Until his rage was spent.

He will comb his hair, trim his beard,
And try to find what happened
To the face in the mirror, the face
He will present, waiting for someone
To smile back, to say the words
That will open the door inside him,
The door that is locked.

BROTHERS

Two years separated them,
Love bound them in a place
No one could enter.

Their young manhood
Was charismatic to others,
Natural to themselves.

A week after his brother's
Death in Vietnam
He joined the Marines.

His killing and medals
Were for his brother
Alive in his thoughts.

Years passed into decades,
His brother's photograph
Stands on the dresser.

Each night as he crossed
The border to sleep
He envisioned his brother,

How they swam in the quarry
Jumping off the highest rock
One beside the other.

THREE BULLETS

Before every mission
He rolled the three bullets
In his large hand,
Then put them in his pocket
For the luck
That would keep him safe.
Thirteen months passed,
A slow blur
Of comrades dying,
His continued luck.
When he boarded
The plane to leave
He still held the bullets.
When he returned to Maine,
The hunting season beginning,
He rolled the bullets
Before entering the woods,
Imagining a sniper
Behind the trees
As he tracked the deer
In the snow.

TURNING AWAY

With his rifle raised
He approached the vulture
Pulling off the remaining meat
From the severed leg.
Was it a Marine's, a VC's?
The vulture refused to rise.
Suddenly he stopped,
Sickened by the killing,
The wounding, the maiming.
"Enjoy it," he said
With an unexpected grin,
Then turned away,
Lowering his rifle that
Seemed double its weight.

ENCOUNTER

His body belongs to an old man,
His spirit rises for another dawn
Leading him to the fields
Outside the town,
Reminding him of the valley
Beyond Da Nang where
He bled the first time—
No enemy waits here.
A coyote on the move
Pauses to stare, its long tail
A curve of the eternal,
Rousing an untouched love inside him.

IN THE VETERAN'S HOME

Blue, red, and yellow
Lights blink on the back
Of the ambulance
Parked near his window
On the first floor
Of the Veteran's home:
The Green Mountains of Vermont
Rest behind it,
The deer sleep in their
Fenced park in front,
Someone is wheeled out on
A gurney in the starless night.
Will he be next?
Eighty years are pressed
Into his field pack
Weighing him down:
Medals, wounds,
And deaths crammed inside.
Every morning he visits
The deer, counting them slowly,
Their beauty immeasurable,
His happiness intact.

Michael Miller's first book, *The Joyful Dark,* was the Editor's Choice winner of The McGovern Prize at Ashland Poetry Press. His third book, *Darkening the Grass,* was a "Must Read" selection of the Massachusetts Book Award in 2013. His poem, "The Different War," 2014 Winner of the W. B. Yeats Poetry Society, was anthologized in Yeats 150 (Lilliput Press, Dublin). His poems have appeared in *The Kenyon Review, The Sewanee Review, The New Republic, The American Scholar, Ontario Review, The Southern Review, Commonweal, Raritan,* and *The Yale Review.* Born in 1940, **Michael Miller** served four years in the Marine Corps. He lives in Amherst, Massachusetts.

www.ingramcontent.com/pod-product-compliance
Lightning Source LLC
Chambersburg PA
CBHW030058170426
43197CB00010B/1583